BUSINESS, TECHNOLOGY AND FINANCE

FINANCIAL LITERACY FORUMS

ISSUES AND VIEWPOINTS ON THE WORKPLACE, PARTNERSHIPS AND GOVERNMENTAL ROLE

BUSINESS, TECHNOLOGY AND FINANCE

Additional books in this series can be found on Nova's website
under the Series tab.

Additional e-books in this series can be found on Nova's website
under the e-book tab.

BUSINESS, TECHNOLOGY AND FINANCE

FINANCIAL LITERACY FORUMS

ISSUES AND VIEWPOINTS ON THE WORKPLACE, PARTNERSHIPS AND GOVERNMENTAL ROLE

CAROLINE HOLLAND
EDITOR

New York

Additional color graphics may be available in the e-book version of this book.

Library of Congress Cataloging-in-Publication Data

ISBN: 978-1-63484-337-9

Published by Nova Science Publishers, Inc. † New York

CONTENTS

PREFACE

Americans today confront an array of challenges in their efforts to achieve and maintain financial security. Financial literacy—the ability to use knowledge and skills to manage financial resources effectively—has thus become increasingly important. Experts have identified the workplace as a potentially effective venue for providing financial education and helping individuals improve their financial decision making. This book discusses the role of the employer in promoting financial literacy; the effectiveness of such efforts; how best to serve low-income and other underserved populations; and the federal government's role in supporting these efforts. The book also discusses needs and priorities in improving financial literacy; roles and responsibilities of, and collaboration among, the government, nonprofit, and private sectors; lessons learned from federal public health and nutrition literacy initiatives; and the Government Accountability Office's potential role in addressing financial literacy issues.

In: Financial Literacy Forums
Editor: Caroline Holland
ISBN: 978-1-63484-337-9

Chapter 1

FINANCIAL LITERACY: THE ROLE OF THE WORKPLACE*

United States Government Accountability Office

WHY GAO CONVENED THIS FORUM

Americans today confront an array of challenges in their efforts to achieve and maintain financial security. Financial literacy—the ability to use knowledge and skills to manage financial resources effectively—has thus become increasingly important. Experts have identified the workplace as a potentially effective venue for providing financial education and helping individuals improve their financial decision making.

On March 17, 2015, GAO convened a select group of leaders and experts for a forum focusing on financial education in the workplace. The participants discussed

- the role of the employer in promoting financial literacy,
- the effectiveness of such efforts,
- how best to serve low-income and other underserved populations, and
- the federal government's role in supporting these efforts.

* This is an edited, reformatted and augmented version of The United States Government Accountability Office publication, GAO-15-639SP, dated July 2015.

- Participants, selected to represent a range of experience and viewpoints, included experts from the private sector, federal government agencies, nongovernmental organizations, and academic institutions. Participants reviewed a draft of this summary, and their comments were incorporated as appropriate. Comments expressed during the proceedings do not necessarily represent the views of all participants, the organizations with which they are affiliated, or GAO.

WHAT PARTICIPANTS SAID

Participants highlighted the following themes during the forum:

- *Employers are well-suited to play a role in promoting financial literacy.* Participants noted that employers already provide information on employee benefits, have key information about employees' lives, and are generally trusted to provide sound financial information and advice.
- *Workplace financial wellness programs should be comprehensive.* These programs should expand beyond the current emphasis on retirement planning and benefits, participants said, to include education on such areas as everyday budgeting and money management, building an emergency savings fund, and understanding the financial impacts of health care.
- *Effective practices can include automatic enrollment in retirement plans, financial health checks, and personalization.* Automatically enrolling new employees into defined contribution plans increases retirement savings, although it may not be appropriate for some workers who have other pressing resource needs. Some participants said that such behavioral approaches should complement, rather than replace, traditional financial education. Other strategies participants cited included providing unbiased information, individualizing education based on employees' unique circumstances, and offering personal financial coaching.
- *Employers should address the needs of traditionally underserved workplace populations.* Participants noted the importance of effectively reaching all employees, including shift workers, contingent workers, low-income employees, and those with different cultural

backgrounds. Strategies included tailoring the content to be relevant and understandable, delivering information though online tools and mobile devices, and leveraging partners, such as unions, churches, and community groups.

- *Additional research and evaluation are needed.* There is limited research on the effectiveness of interventions not related to retirement savings. Some participants said more randomized experiments are needed to truly assess what works, and a standard set of benchmarks for measuring effectiveness would be useful.
- *Financial education benefits employers, but demonstrating return on investment is key.* Financial education can benefit employers through increased employee productivity and improved recruiting and retention, but employers expect solid, independent evidence of these benefits to justify their investment.
- *Federal agencies should build on efforts to support workplace financial education.* Some participants said federal agencies should clarify rules for private sector employers on the financial advice they can give employees, and others wanted increased federal support for research. Other participants encouraged federal agencies to continue their efforts to educate their own employees and build partnerships with the nonprofit and private sectors.

INTRODUCTION

Americans today confront an array of challenges in their efforts to achieve and maintain financial security. From economic hardship experienced during the recent recession, to the increasing responsibility to pay for health care and accumulate retirement savings, individuals and families must navigate a number of issues as they make choices that will have long-term effects. Financial literacy—the ability to use knowledge and skills to manage financial resources effectively—has thus become increasingly important.

Experts have identified the workplace as potentially being a particularly effective venue for providing financial education and helping individuals improve their financial decision making. Employers have the potential to reach large numbers of adults in a cost-effective manner at a place where they make important financial decisions regarding, for example, retirement, life and health insurance, and specialized savings accounts for child care and medical expenses. Further, the Bureau of Consumer Financial Protection (known as the Consumer Financial Protection Bureau) and others have conducted research indicating that workplace financial education programs can result in employees who are better able to manage financial stresses and are more productive.[1]

However, the extent to which private and public sector entities offer employee financial education varies. Many employers offer information on retirement and other benefits, sometimes to meet federal requirements. For example, the Employee Retirement Income Security Act of 1974 requires employers to provide certain information to participants in pension and other employee benefit plans about plan features.[2] In addition, the Office of Personnel Management requires federal agencies to develop plans for educating their employees on retirement planning.[3]

Some employers have developed comprehensive programs aimed at overall improvement in employees' financial health. These programs— often called financial wellness programs—can parallel the physical wellness programs employers have established to encourage exercise and healthy food and lifestyle choices. Such comprehensive, or holistic, financial wellness programs may offer employees assistance with budgeting, emergency savings, and credit management, in addition to the traditional information and assistance provided for retirement and health benefits.

Researchers have made progress in identifying effective financial education programs and other types of financial interventions. For example, a substantial body of research has focused on interventions to increase employees' retirement savings.[4] However, there are important gaps in the understanding of how employers can best effect positive changes in other aspects of their employees' financial behavior.

The federal government plays an important role in supporting financial literacy generally, and also has a role in supporting financial education in the workplace. In 2014, we reported that federal agencies had 12 significant financial literacy programs or activities under way.[5] For example, the Consumer Financial Protection Bureau has a broad mandate to support financial literacy and education for all consumers, and other agencies, such as the Social Security Administration, focus on specific topics or audiences. The multiagency Financial Literacy and Education Commission is responsible for coordinating federal financial literacy efforts and developing a national strategy to promote financial literacy.[6] Some federal agencies, such as the Department of Labor and the Internal Revenue Service, influence private sector workplace financial education efforts, such as through enforcing certain pension plan requirements. In addition, federal agencies, including GAO, have initiatives to educate their own employees.

GAO plays a number of roles in addressing financial literacy. Our reports and testimonies at congressional hearings have provided oversight of federal financial literacy programs and activities and have integrated financial literacy issues into broader reviews of such areas as credit card products, elder financial exploitation, and fraudulent foreclosure rescue schemes. [7] In addition, we have implemented an internal financial literacy program for our own employees, including classroom-based training, a speaker series, and other resources. GAO also has facilitated knowledge transfer among key players in the arena of financial literacy, including through prior Comptroller General forums in 2004 and 2011.[8]

On March 17, 2015, GAO convened a group of 20 financial literacy leaders and experts for a forum focusing on financial education in the workplace. The participants included representatives from the private sector, federal government agencies, nongovernmental organizations, and academic institutions, and were selected to represent a range of viewpoints and backgrounds. In the first session of the day-long forum, participants discussed the role of the employer in promoting financial literacy. The second session addressed the effectiveness of interventions to improve employees' financial decision making. The third session focused on the challenges associated with addressing the needs of low-income, blue-collar, service, and shift workers who may not work in an office environment or receive comprehensive benefits and who may change jobs frequently. In the fourth session, participants discussed the role of the federal government in educating its own employees and facilitating private sector efforts. The participants completed the day by identifying what they believed were the key themes generated by the forum.

The following is a summary of the discussion among the forum's participants. The summary attempts to capture the ideas and themes that emerged at the forum and the collective discussion of participants at the sessions. The summary does not necessarily represent the views of the organizations, including GAO, whose representatives participated in the forum. The forum was structured so that participants could comment on issues openly, although not all participants commented on all topics. Participants were given the opportunity to comment on a draft of this summary.

We conducted our work from August 2014 to July 2015 in accordance with all sections of GAO's Quality Assurance Framework that are relevant to our objectives. The framework requires that we plan and perform the engagement to obtain sufficient, appropriate evidence to meet our stated objectives and to discuss any limitations in our work. We believe that the information and data obtained, and the analysis conducted, provide a reasonable basis for any findings and conclusions.

Appendix I provides the forum agenda, and appendix II provides a list of the participants. Appendix III is a description of our scope and methodology, and appendix IV lists related GAO products.

I wish to thank all of the participants for their thoughtful contributions to our discussion of financial education in the workplace. The discussion enhanced our understanding and provided valuable suggestions for ways to make progress on this important issue.

Gene L. Dodaro
Comptroller General of the United States
July 7, 2015

* * *

FINANCIAL LITERACY: HIGHLIGHTS OF THE FORUM DISCUSSION

On March 17, 2015, GAO convened a forum to discuss financial education in the workplace. Twenty participants discussed the role of employers in improving employees' financial decision making and wellness; the effectiveness of various interventions; how to address the needs of workplace populations traditionally underserved by financial education; and the role of the federal government in supporting these efforts. The following summarizes the collective discussion of the forum participants.

Employers Are Well-Suited to Play a Role in Promoting Financial Literacy

Forum participants cited several reasons why employers are well-suited to play a role in improving the financial literacy and wellness of their employees.

- *Employers already provide information about benefits.* Participants generally noted that employers, in both the private and public sectors, already provide retirement and health benefits and information about those benefits to their employees, and thus are well-positioned to provide information more broadly on financial topics. Several participants noted that some employers, in both the private and public sectors, already have broad financial education or financial wellness programs in place.

- *Employers have key information about employees' lives.* Two participants noted that employers are well-suited to target timely and appropriate financial education to employees because they already possess key information about their employees' financial lives—such as salary and benefits and timing of key life events, such as marriage or the birth of a child. For example, one participant cited an employer that combines notification of pay increases with suggestions on using those funds to increase savings or pay down debt.
- *Employees trust employers to provide sound financial information.* Employees often trust the financial information or advice that they get from their employers, believing—rightly or wrongly—that employers have vetted the information they provide, according to several participants. Four participants observed that employers generally are perceived as acting in their employees' interest when offering financial information, although one participant noted that some employees may be wary of employers intruding into their personal lives. Another participant noted that employers can be an important source of financial information because many people otherwise seek out such information from friends and family, whom they perceive as ethical and unbiased, even when they may doubt their competence.
- *Challenges remain for some employers.* However, several participants acknowledged the challenges faced by some employers in addressing employees' financial wellness. One participant noted that smaller companies in particular may not view financial education programs as an urgent priority compared with other competing claims on limited resources. In addition, a few participants said that many employers remain skeptical of the benefits of financial education to them or their employees, and one noted that some employers do not view financial education as their responsibility.

Workplace Financial Wellness Programs Should Be Comprehensive

Traditionally, workplace financial education has focused primarily on retirement and health benefits. However, forum participants generally advocated expanding such efforts to cover a more comprehensive set of issues, recommending that employers do the following:

- *Educate on everyday money management.* Several participants noted that some employees may need help with budgeting and basic money management, as well as addressing high-cost debt and improving their credit records. Two participants mentioned that employees may need help learning how to avoid self-destructive mistakes and predatory practices.
- *Help employees prepare for financial emergencies.* Several participants highlighted the importance of helping employees understand the need to build up an emergency savings fund. One recommended that employers also assist interested employees in setting up or allocating a portion of their paychecks to such an account.
- *Incorporate information on the financial impacts of health care.* Four participants emphasized educating employees on the issues around health care expenses. They noted that the growth in medical costs and health insurance options and the role of tax-preferred health savings accounts have made health care an essential and complex part of financial planning.

Effective Practices Can Include Automatic Enrollment in Retirement Plans, Financial Health Checks, and Personalization

Forum participants identified a number of employer practices that research and experience have shown can help employees improve their overall financial wellness. Participants said that not all strategies are appropriate for all workplaces but that several techniques could work well in a number of environments.

- *Use automatic enrollment as appropriate.* Several participants noted that automatically enrolling new employees into employers' defined contribution plans has been proven widely effective at increasing retirement contributions across diverse populations. Some participants did caution that this approach may not be appropriate for all employees, noting that a default savings contribution (such as 5 percent of salary) may be too low for some employees (such as those nearing retirement) and too high for others (such as those having trouble making ends meet, paying down high-cost debt, or trying to build up an emergency savings fund). Two participants noted that in some workplaces, 30 percent to 40 percent of employees who were automatically enrolled in a retirement account had taken a loan against that account, suggesting that the default contribution rate was too high.
- *Do not use behavioral approaches in isolation.* At least three participants said that behavioral approaches such as automatic enrollment should complement, rather than replace, traditional financial education. Several participants said that well-run traditional financial education methods—such as seminars and personal financial coaching—also are effective tools for changing behavior.
- *Provide unbiased information and advice.* Three participants stressed that employers should ensure that the financial information they provide is unbiased and avoids even the appearance of conflicts of interest. For that reason, three participants cautioned against using retirement and health plan providers to deliver financial education to employees. Another participant noted that it can be challenging to ensure that third-party advisors brought in by the employer are working in employees' best interests because they may be trying to sell a product.
- *Assess employees' financial health and literacy.* Some participants advocated employer programs that periodically assess employees' financial situations and goals, which can pinpoint how best to provide assistance and help employees set priorities. One participant noted that such assessments can be important because many people have limited financial knowledge but do not know it, and three participants cited research demonstrating that many employees do not understand basic concepts like compound interest or insurance deductibles.
- *Personalize information.* Employers can use information on employees' income, life events, and participation in retirement and

health plans to personalize the advice that they provide. Some participants noted that employees nearing retirement require different information from those just starting their careers. One participant described how his organization uses employee data to tailor financial education messages to specific individuals as they experience certain life events.

- *Consider personal financial coaching.* Three participants recommended that employers provide access to one-on-one financial coaches who can help employees understand their priorities and then take action on those priorities. Participants discussed the importance of making it easy for participants to convert knowledge to action—for example, by helping employees set up emergency savings accounts, rather than just encouraging them to do so.

Employers Should Address the Needs of Traditionally Underserved Workplace Populations

Employer-based financial education has tended to focus on white-collar workers with retirement plans rather than blue-collar, service, and shift workers who may not work in an office environment or receive comprehensive benefits and who may change jobs frequently, noted several participants. They suggested ways of tailoring the content, delivery mechanisms, or approach of financial education to reach a diverse workforce.

- *Vary the topics as appropriate.* Several participants said the topics covered in financial education must be tailored to the needs of different types of workers. For example, retirement planning may not be a priority for many low-income workers, who may need assistance on how to manage day-to-day expenses or pay down high-cost debt.
- *Make content accessible.* Several participants said that employers should make sure the content of financial education is easy to understand for all populations. One participant discussed translating educational materials into other languages and ensuring they are culturally relevant to diverse communities. Participants also encouraged using plain language instead of technical terms like compound interest.
- *Tailor delivery mechanisms.* Participants cited challenges that can arise in delivering financial education to employees who are dispersed

geographically or may work in a retail or factory setting, or out in the field, rather than in an office with a computer. Four participants said that social media and mobile technology can be effective ways of distributing information because they are scalable, inexpensive, and socially accepted, noting that even most workers without computer access now use mobile devices. One participant cited his company's use of text messages to reach employees with financial education messages. However, two participants cautioned that employees already receive a lot of information and may ignore information if they receive too much. Three participants advocated centralized online financial education resources for employees—or their family decision makers—to access at any time on any device. Three participants highlighted the need to compensate shift workers, in particular, for the time they spend in employer-provided financial education programs.

- *Leverage trusted messengers and external partners.* Six participants encouraged using trusted coworkers and other peers to provide or facilitate assistance on financial matters. Two participants said that their organizations trained employees to explain financial information to their colleagues, and another suggested using recently retired employees for this purpose. Four participants advocated leveraging external parties such as community groups and church groups, or using unions to expand outreach to underserved populations. One participant suggested bringing community groups that offer free tax assistance into the workplace during tax season, in part to help ensure that lower-income employees take advantage of the Earned Income Tax Credit.[9]

Additional Research and Evaluation Are Needed

Participants discussed additional research and evaluation needed to determine effective means of improving workplace financial education and employee financial wellness.

- *Nonretirement issues and ways to motivate behavioral change are among the research priorities.* Participants emphasized that while there is much research on interventions related to retirement savings, there is less information available on the effectiveness of interventions related to other financial issues, such as avoiding high-cost debt and managing health care expenses. In addition, three participants highlighted the need for more research on effectively motivating individuals to engage in positive financial behaviors.

- *Employers should consider benchmarks for measuring effectiveness.* Several participants advocated development of a widely accepted definition of success, or a standard framework or set of goals, against which employers can measure the effectiveness of their interventions. Some participants noted that it is far easier to measure some outcomes—such as enrollment in a retirement or health plan—than others for which the employer does not maintain data, such as employees' levels of savings and debt. They also cautioned that the definitions of success may not always be obvious— for example, while increasing retirement plan contributions is generally considered a positive goal, it may not be the most appropriate action for all employees in all situations.
- *Randomized controlled trials and user testing are valuable.* Three participants highlighted the importance of determining effectiveness through randomized controlled trials with, as feasible, large representative samples and appropriate metrics.[10] In addition, two participants said that testing specific financial programs on their intended audiences can be a powerful tool to refine the programs and assess their clarity, format, and effectiveness. One participant noted that Internet-based interventions are well-suited for simple randomized experiments, such as testing two versions of a communication to determine which one prompts more people to take action.
- *Lessons from other fields and partnerships can aid research.* Two participants noted that research on influencing health and nutrition behaviors can apply to influencing financial behaviors. One participant noted that research on the use of monetary incentives to change eating behaviors can be instructive for interventions designed to affect financial decision making. Several participants encouraged greater cooperation and partnership between employers and researchers to improve understanding of which workplace financial education interventions work best.

Financial Education Benefits Employers, but Demonstrating Return on Investment Is Key

Most participants said that workplace financial education benefits both employees and employers. However, while human resources managers often recognize these benefits, they must do a better job making the case for financial education to senior executives, who typically want to see evidence of a return on investment in these efforts.

- *Reducing stress about finances can improve productivity.* A key benefit of workplace financial wellness programs, said several participants, is improved productivity due to reduced employee stress about financial matters, a point that was noted in a recent report by the Consumer Financial Protection Bureau.[11] Two participants cited recent surveys that found that employees typically spend several hours per week addressing financial issues during work hours and that poor financial planning by employees has affected their performance on the job.
- *Financial education can aid recruiting and retention.* Two participants said that workplace financial education can improve employees' engagement, loyalty, and retention, and can be an attractive recruiting tool. One participant said that his organization's financial health and wellness programs had helped attract and retain employees.
- *Independent analysis of benefits is lacking.* Participants generally agreed that employers want to see a "business case" for financial wellness programs—that is, evidence demonstrating a return on their investment in such programs. Two participants commented that while some studies have shown a positive return on investment, these studies generally focused on small-scale experiments or were published by service providers viewed as potentially biased. As a result, many participants said that independent, third-party assessments of the return on investment of employer financial wellness programs are important.

Federal Agencies Should Build on Efforts to Support Workplace Financial Education

Participants were asked how the federal government can support private sector employers' financial education efforts, as well as ways that federal agencies can further educate their own employees.

- *Clarify rules about employer-provided financial advice and guidance.* Several participants said they believed it would be helpful for the federal government to provide additional clarification about the difference between educating plan participants and providing them with investment advice.[12] Two participants said that fear of legal liability for breaching their fiduciary duties has made some employers reluctant to directly offer employees guidance on which retirement plan options may be most appropriate based on their specific financial situation. They said that many employers instead rely on third-party vendors—such as firms managing an employer's retirement or health plan—to advise employees, despite the fact that these firms may not always work in employees' best interest.
- *Conduct or fund additional research and data collection.* Several participants encouraged increased federal support for research and data collection on workplace financial education. [13] Three participants praised the Social Security Administration's prior support of financial literacy research, with one participant commenting that the support had produced some of the top research in this field and recommending its funding be resumed.[14] One participant also highlighted the value of the Consumer Financial Protection Bureau's research on defining financial well-being and financial capability, and the Department of the Treasury's Financial Empowerment Innovation Fund.[15] Two participants believed the federal government could take the lead on developing a uniform data set that could be used broadly for research.
- *Continue partnerships with the nonprofit and private sectors.* Some participants encouraged federal agencies to continue or expand their partnerships with other government entities and with nonprofits and private sector organizations. One participant highlighted the efforts of the President's Advisory Council on Financial Capability for Young Americans and its role in making connections with employers, nonprofits, and local service providers. [16] This participant noted the council's interest in reaching young people during their

summer employment to teach them about savings and other financial skills. Two participants highlighted the Department of the Treasury's *my*RA (*my* Retirement Account) program, which aims to work with employers to offer basic retirement savings products to employees whose employers do not offer retirement plans.[17] A few participants suggested that federal agencies should consider additional ways of publicly recognizing employers that have broad-based financial education programs.

- *Reduce the regulatory burden to free up resources.* Three private sector participants expressed the opinion that the general burden of federal regulation and reporting requirements served to divert resources that employers could otherwise use for efforts like financial education. One of these participants noted additionally that simplifying the complex rules governing employer-provided benefits would reduce the amount of financial education employees require to understand them.
- *Build on existing efforts to educate federal employees.* Participants discussed federal agencies' efforts to provide financial education to their own employees. One participant encouraged wider use by federal agencies of promising practices and policies for workplace financial wellness that were identified by the Consumer Financial Protection Bureau.[18] In addition, four participants said that federal agencies should provide the Thrift Savings Plan with their employees' e-mail addresses to facilitate communication and education.[19] One participant noted that federal agencies may benefit from the results of the Financial Literacy and Education Commission's review of how to reach employees with financial education early in their careers.

APPENDIX I: FORUM AGENDA

Financial Literacy: The Role of the Workplace

A Forum Convened by Comptroller General of the United States Gene L. Dodaro U.S. Government Accountability Office

Tuesday, March 17, 2015

	Agenda	
8:30 a.m	Continental Breakfast	McCarl Room
9:00 a.m.	Opening Session -Welcome -Personal introductions -Overview of agenda	Staats Briefing Room Gene L. Dodaro Comptroller General of the United States
9:30 a.m.	The Role of Employers in Providing Workplace Financial Education	Moderators: Gene L. Dodaro Andrew Stavisky Senior Methodologist GAO
10:45 a.m.	Break	
11:00 a.m.	What Works?	Moderators: Susan Offutt Chief Economist GAO David Dornisch Senior Methodologist GAO
12:15 p.m.	Lunch	
1:15 p.m.	Addressing Employees Underserved by Workplace Financial Education	Moderators: Barbara D. Bovbjerg Managing Director Education, Workforce, and Income Security, GAO Andrew Stavisky
2:30 p.m.	Break	
2:45 p.m.	The Federal Government's Role in Facilitating Workplace Financial Education	Moderators: Orice Williams Brown Managing Director Financial Markets and Community Investment
		David Dornisch
3:45 p.m	Concluding Observations and Discussion of Potential Topics of Future Financial Literacy Forums	Moderators: Daniel Garcia-Diaz Director Financial Markets and Community Investment
		David Dornisch
4:15 p.m.	Adjournment	

APPENDIX II: FORUM PARTICIPANTS

Ted Beck	President and CEO National Endowment for Financial Education
Saurabh Bhargava	Assistant Professor of Economics, Department of Social and Decision Sciences Carnegie Mellon University
Phyllis C. Borzi	Assistant Secretary of Labor, Employee Benefits Security Administration U.S. Department of Labor
Barbara D. Bovbjerg	Managing Director, Education, Workforce, and Income Security GAO
Orice Williams Brown	Managing Director, Financial Markets and Community Investment GAO
Liz Davidson	Founder and CEO Financial Finesse, Inc.
Katy Davis	Vice President ideas42
Gene L. Dodaro	Comptroller General of the United States GAO
David Dornisch	Senior Methodologist GAO
Debra Golding	Deputy Director, Consumer and Compliance Outreach and Education U.S. Department of Labor
Daniel Garcia-Diaz	Director, Financial Markets and Community Investment GAO
Kevin T. Hanney	Director, Pension Investments United Technologies Corporation
Aaron J. Harding	Director, Financial Education and Wellness Practice PricewaterhouseCoopers LLP
Gail Hillebrand	Associate Director of Consumer Education & Engagement Consumer Financial Protection Bureau
Angela Hung	Director, Center for Financial and Economic Decision Making RAND Corporation
Melissa S. Koide	Deputy Assistant Secretary, Office of Consumer Policy

	U.S. Department of the Treasury
Barbara Kontje	Director, Retirement Americas & Smart Saving American Express Company
Gregory T. Long	Executive Director Federal Retirement Thrift Investment Board
Annamaria Lusardi	Denit Trust Chair of Economics and Accountancy The George Washington University School of Business
Susan Offutt	Chief Economist GAO
Louisa Quittman	Director, Financial Education, Office of Consumer Policy U.S. Department of Treasury
Chad Ryan	Senior Director, Global Retirement and Financial Wellness PepsiCo, Inc.
Maximilian Schmeiser	Senior Economist Board of Governors of the Federal Reserve System
Brian Silva	Chair, Board of Directors Society for Human Resource Management
Andrew Stavisky	Senior Methodologist GAO
Stephen Wendel	Principal Scientist HelloWallet
Rosemary Williams	Deputy Assistant Secretary (Military Community and Family Policy) U.S. Department of Defense

APPENDIX III: SCOPE AND METHODOLOGY

This report summarizes discussions at the GAO forum, Financial Literacy: The Role of the Workplace, which took place on March 17, 2015. We selected and invited participants with a wide range of experience and expertise to attend the forum, which consisted of four topic-based sessions and a final wrap-up session. We then prepared a summary of the discussions and submitted a draft of that summary to participants for their review. We incorporated participants' comments, as appropriate. The following sections describe our approach to the forum and summary in greater detail.

FORUM PARTICIPANT SELECTION

The 20 participants included individuals affiliated with private sector entities, federal government agencies, nongovernmental organizations, and academic institutions, and they were selected to encompass a range of experience and viewpoints. We began our selection process by reviewing prior GAO work on financial literacy and related issues. We then surveyed recent literature on financial literacy topics and recent financial literacy symposiums and conferences to identify individuals with relevant expertise. We also had discussions with experts in the area of financial literacy about individuals who have been at the forefront of recent research and trends in financial literacy and implementation of workplace financial education programs.

We selected participants to represent a mix of the following:

- organization types that include private sector employers, federal agencies, nongovernmental organizations, and academic research environments;
- individuals with experience managing or implementing financial education initiatives, particularly those in the workplace; and
- individuals with experience conducting research related to workplace financial education or financial decision making, or with familiarity with the relevant body of research.

The group of 20 participants we assembled included 6 individuals from the private sector, 7 from federal government agencies, 3 from nongovernmental organizations, and 4 academic researchers. (An additional 7 individuals from GAO participated in at least one session.)

COMPTROLLER GENERAL FORUM

The day-long forum on March 17, 2015 consisted of four sessions ranging from 60 to 75 minutes each, with a final 30-minute wrap-up session. Each session was moderated by two GAO staff members—a senior subject-matter expert and a methodologist who served as facilitator. The forum was structured so that participants could comment on issues openly, although not all participants commented on all topics. The first session addressed the role of the employer in promoting financial literacy. The second session addressed the effectiveness of workplace financial education and financial wellness interventions. The third session focused on the needs of populations traditionally underserved by workplace financial education, such as blue-collar, service, and shift workers who may not work in an office environment or receive comprehensive benefits and who may change jobs frequently. The fourth session addressed ways federal agencies could support private sector efforts, and ways that agencies could improve their own internal financial literacy and education programs for federal employees, including military servicemembers and their families. In the final 30-minute session, each participant had the opportunity to identify key themes generated during the forum sessions.

Forum Summary Report

Following the forum, we drafted a summary of the report and submitted it to participants for their review. In addition, two participants contacted us after the forum to clarify certain points and expand on certain topics. We incorporated participants' comments into the final report as appropriate.

The summary does not necessarily represent the views of the organizations with which the forum participants are affiliated, including GAO. The participants were informed that we would not directly identify individuals or their affiliations in association with specific comments without their permission, and this report does not do so.

We conducted our work from August 2014 to July 2015 in accordance with all sections of GAO's Quality Assurance Framework that are relevant to our objectives. The framework requires that we plan and perform the engagement to obtain sufficient, appropriate evidence to meet our stated objectives and to discuss any limitations in our work. We believe that the information and data obtained, and the analysis conducted, provide a reasonable basis for any findings and conclusions.

Appendix IV: Related GAO Products

401(K) Plans: Improvements Can Be Made to Better Protect Participants in Managed Accounts. GAO-14-310. Washington, D.C.: June 25, 2014.

Financial Literacy: Overview of Federal Activities, Programs, and Challenges. GAO-14-556T. Washington, D.C.: April 30, 2014.

Retirement Security: Challenges for Those Claiming Social Security Benefits Early and New Health Coverage Options. GAO-14-311. Washington, D.C.: April 23, 2014.

Private Pensions: Clarity of Required Reports and Disclosures Could Be Improved. GAO-14-92. Washington, D.C.: November 21, 2013.

401(K) Plans: Labor and IRS Could Improve the Rollover Process for Participants. GAO-13-30. Washington, D.C.: March 7, 2013.

Financial Literacy: Overlap of Programs Suggests There May Be Opportunities for Consolidation. GAO-12-588. Washington, D.C.: July 23, 2012.

Financial Literacy: Enhancing the Effectiveness of the Federal Government's Role. GAO-12-636T. Washington, D.C.: April 26, 2012.

Highlights of a Forum: Financial Literacy: Strengthening Partnerships in Challenging Times. GAO-12-299SP. Washington, D.C.: February 9, 2012.

Financial Literacy: A Federal Certification Process for Providers Would Pose Challenges. GAO-11-614. Washington, D.C.: June 28, 2011.

Financial Literacy: The Federal Government's Role in Empowering Americans to Make Sound Financial Choices. GAO-11-504T. Washington, D.C.: April 12, 2011.

Consumer Finance: Factors Affecting the Financial Literacy of Individuals with Limited English Proficiency. GAO-10-518. Washington, D.C.: May 21, 2010.

End Notes

[1] Such research is described in Consumer Financial Protection Bureau, Financial Wellness at Work: A Review of Promising Practices and Policies (Washington, D.C.: August 2014), pp. 12-24. Accessed June 16, 2015. http://www.consumerfinance.gov/reports/financialwellness-at-work/

[2] Pub. L. No. 93-406, 88 Stat. 829 (codified as amended at 29 U.S.C. §§ 1001-1461). The Employee Retirement Income Security Act of 1974 establishes requirements for most private sector employee benefit plans. Because qualified employee benefit plans receive preferential tax treatment, the Department of Labor shares oversight and enforcement responsibilities over such plans with the Internal Revenue Service.

[3] The Thrift Savings Plan Open Elections Act of 2004 required the Office of Personnel Management, in consultation with the Federal Retirement Thrift Investment Board, to develop and implement a retirement financial literacy and education strategy for federal

employees as part of the retirement training offered under 5 U.S.C. § 8350. Pub. L. No. 108-469, § 2, 118 Stat. 3891, 3892 (2004) (codified at 5 U.S.C. § 8350 note).

[4] We reviewed the body of research on the effectiveness of financial literacy programs in GAO, Financial Literacy: A Federal Certification Process for Providers Would Pose Challenges, GAO-11-614 (Washington, D.C.: June 28, 2011), pp. 6-15.

[5] GAO, Financial Literacy: Overview of Federal Activities, Programs, and Challenges, GAO-14-556T (Washington, D.C.: Apr. 30, 2014).

[6] T he multiagency Financial Literacy and Education Commission was created by Congress in the 2003 Financial Literacy and Education Improvement Act, Pub. L. No. 108-159, Tit. V, § 513, 117 Stat. 1952, 2003 (2003) (codified as amended at 20 U.S.C. § 9702). The Commission is charged with, among other things, developing a national strategy to promote financial literacy and education, coordinating federal efforts, and identifying areas of overlap and duplication. See 20 U.S.C. §§ 9702(b), 9703(f).

[7] For example, see GAO, Credit Cards: Consumer Costs for Debt Protection Products Can Be Substantial Relative to Benefits but Are Not a Focus of Regulatory Oversight, GAO-11-311 (Washington, D.C.: Mar. 25, 2011); Elder Justice: National Strategy Needed to Effectively Combat Elder Financial Exploitation, GAO-13-110 (Washington, D.C.: Nov. 15, 2012); and Financial Crime: Foreclosure Rescue Schemes Have Become More Complex, and Efforts to Combat Them Continue, GAO-14-17 (Washington, D.C.: Oct. 29, 2013).

[8] GAO, Highlights of a Forum: Financial Literacy: Strengthening Partnerships in Challenging Times, GAO-12-299SP (Washington, D.C.: Feb. 9, 2012); and Highlights of a GAO Forum: The Federal Government's Role in Improving Financial Literacy, GAO-05-93SP (Washington, D.C.: Nov. 15, 2004).

[9] The Earned Income Tax Credit is a refundable credit available to low-income workers, meaning that working taxpayers who qualify may receive an income tax refund if the amount of the credit is greater than their tax liability. See GAO, Advanced Earned Income Tax Credit: Low Use and Small Dollars Paid Impede IRS's Efforts to Reduce High Noncompliance. GAO-07-1110 (Washington, D.C.: Aug. 10, 2007).

[10] Randomized controlled trials (or randomized experiments) measure the impact of an intervention by comparing outcomes for participants who were randomly assigned either to a group receiving the intervention or to a nonparticipating control group, in an effort to control for any systematic difference between the groups that could account for a difference in their outcomes.

[11] Consumer Financial Protection Bureau, Financial Wellness at Work.

[12] The Employee Retirement Income Security Act of 1974 requires plan fiduciaries, including plan sponsors, to act solely in the interest of plan participants. 29 U.S.C.§ 1104(a). The Department of Labor recently published a proposed rule on the act's definition of fiduciary that would, among other things, clarify the distinction between fiduciary investment advice and nonfiduciary investment information and education. Definition of the Term "Fiduciary"; Conflict of Interest Rule—Retirement Investment Advice, 80 Fed. Reg. 21,928, 12,939 (Apr. 20, 2015).

[13] We have previously reported on the wide range of research and evaluation related to financial education that is conducted or supported by federal agencies. See GAO, Financial Literacy: Overlap of Programs Suggests There May Be Opportunities for Consolidation. GAO-12-588 (Washington, D.C.: July 23, 2012), pp. 27-37.

[14] In 2009, the Social Security Administration established a Financial Literacy Research Consortium that funded 63 research projects at three academic centers on a range of

consumer financial behavior and retirement savings issues. The program did not receive funding after fiscal year 2010.

[15] The Department of the Treasury has awarded contracts under the Financial Empowerment Innovation Fund to develop, test, and evaluate new ways to "empower Americans with their finances and help them access safe and affordable financial products and services."

[16] The President's Advisory Council on Financial Capability for Young Americans was created within the Department of the Treasury by Executive Order in June 2013. The council advises the President and the Secretary of the Treasury on how to promote financial capability among young Americans and encourage building the financial capability of young people at an early stage in schools, families, communities, and the workplace and through use of technology. Exec. Order No. 13,646, 78 Fed. Reg. 39,159 (June 25, 2013).

[17] The Department of the Treasury describes myRA as a retirement savings account designed to be simple, safe, and affordable. The accounts have no maintenance fees or minimum contribution and the investment is backed by the United States Treasury. See https://myra.gov/.

[18] Consumer Financial Protection Bureau, Financial Wellness at Work.

[19] The Thrift Savings Plan is a retirement savings and investment plan for federal civilian employees and members of the uniformed services established by Congress in the Federal Employees' Retirement System Act of 1986. Pub. L. No 99-335, § 101, 100 Stat. 514, 541-557 (codified as amended at 5 U.S.C. §§ 8431-8440f). It offers retirement savings opportunities and tax benefits similar to those available to private sector employees through 401(k) plans.

In: Financial Literacy Forums
Editor: Caroline Holland
ISBN: 978-1-63484-337-9

Chapter 2

FINANCIAL LITERACY: STRENGTHENING PARTNERSHIPS IN CHALLENGING TIMES*

United States Government Accountability Office

WHY GAO CONVENED THIS FORUM

Giving Americans the information they need to make effective financial decisions can be key to their wellbeing, and to the country's economic health. The recent financial crisis— during which many borrowers did not fully understand the risks associated with alternative mortgage products— underscored the need to improve individuals' financial literacy. Further, economic, demographic, and technological trends that have affected the need for financial literacy continue, including the retirement of the baby boomers; the emergence of new financial products; and increasing costs for health care, higher education, and retirement. GAO convened a forum on October 20, 2011, to discuss (1) needs and priorities in improving financial literacy; (2) roles and responsibilities of, and collaboration among, the government, nonprofit, and private sectors; (3) lessons learned from federal public health and nutrition literacy initiatives; and (4) GAO's potential role in addressing financial literacy issues.

* This is an edited, reformatted and augmented version of a report, GAO-12-299SP, issued by the Government Accountability Office, dated February 9, 2012.

Forum participants included representatives of federal, state, and local government organizations; academic experts; nonprofit practitioners; and representatives from the private sector. Comments expressed during the proceedings do not necessarily represent the views of all participants, the organizations they represent, or GAO. Participants were given the opportunity to comment on a draft of this summary.

WHAT PARTICIPANTS SAID

Participants highlighted the following themes during the forum:

*Focus on key populations***.** Participants discussed a number of areas that should be the most sustained focus of the nation's financial literacy efforts in the coming years. Among other areas, efforts should target kindergarten through 12th grade education; the workplace; the preretirement years; and special populations that may be particularly vulnerable, including low-income communities, the Hispanic community, and older Americans. Materials should be tailored as appropriate to meet these populations' characteristics and circumstances.

*Identify the most effective approaches and target efforts accordingly***.** More research is needed to identify the most effective approaches to improving financial knowledge and behavior. Targeting products appropriately, improving delivery mechanisms, and leveraging technology are also important.

*Enhance the role of employers in improving their employees' financial literacy***.** Employers have a key role to play in improving the financial literacy of their employees—for example, by encouraging them to save for emergencies and retirement. Further, financial literacy stakeholders need to do more to persuade employers of the business benefits of supporting healthy financial behaviors by employees.

*Leverage the unique role of the federal government***.** The federal government has a unique role to play in promoting greater financial literacy. For example, the government can use its convening power and other tools to draw attention to the topic, take advantage of existing connections with certain populations, and make certain legal and regulatory changes to support greater financial literacy.

Increase coordination and partnerships within and across levels of government and different sectors. Opportunities exist to further increase coordination and partnerships among entities involved in financial literacy.

Such efforts could help federal, state, and local government agencies; private sector entities; and nonprofits conserve scarce resources and reduce any duplication of effort.

Identify lessons from other initiatives designed to improve consumer behaviors. Financial literacy practitioners can learn from efforts in other fields, such as health and nutrition, that have sought to educate consumers and influence their behavior. Participants discussed similar challenges, such as the difficulty of influencing people to change their behaviors and the possibility of developing a financial literacy equivalent of the Department of Agriculture's "MyPlate" nutrition graphic.

Participants also discussed ideas for GAO and the Comptroller General to support or raise awareness about financial literacy or partner with others to do so. Among other ideas, they said that GAO could help in efforts to identify the best programs and methods for improving financial literacy, develop a financial literacy initiative for GAO employees that could serve as a potential model for other government agencies, and identify opportunities for federal agencies to leverage existing distribution channels to provide additional financial education.

INTRODUCTION

Giving Americans the information they need to make effective financial decisions can be key to their well-being, as well as to the economic health of our nation. Much has been written and said about the ongoing need to improve our country's level of financial literacy, which is sometimes also referred to as financial capability, and the recent financial crisis has underscorped that need.[1] For example, many borrowers did not fully understand the risks associated with alternative mortgage products that provided them with the ability to purchase homes that ultimately they could not afford. Further, several economic, demographic, and technological trends that affect the need for financial literacy continue, including the retirement of the baby boomers, the emergence of new financial products, and the increasing costs of health care, higher education, and retirement. Given the current economic environment, limited financial literacy can pose barriers to prosperity and higher standards of living. At the same time, however, increasing fiscal constraints at government agencies, particularly with regard to discretionary spending, may limit the resources available for financial literacy efforts.

Much has changed since 2004, when GAO last held a forum on financial literacy.[2] The federal government's multiagency Financial Literacy and Education Commission has now been in place for more than 7 years.[3] In 2010, Congress created the Bureau of Consumer Financial Protection, adding a new player to the mix of federal agencies involved in financial literacy. The bureau will be responsible for, among other things, developing and implementing a strategy to improve consumers' financial literacy and help them access financial counseling and information about such topics as credit products, savings, educational expenses, and wealth building. And a wide variety of organizations continue to provide financial education for consumers, including nonprofit, community-based organizations; consumer advocacy organizations; financial services companies; trade associations; employers; and local, state, and federal government entities.

Notwithstanding these efforts, relatively few financial education programs have been evaluated for effectiveness, and even fewer have undergone assessments that actually measure the programs' impact on participants' behavior, rather than just their knowledge, understanding, or intent. Financial education is not the only approach to improving financial behavior. Alternative strategies and mechanisms, sometimes in conjunction with financial education, have also been successful. In particular, insights from behavioral economists that recognize the realities of human psychology have been used to design successful strategies to assist consumers in reaching financial goals without compromising their ability to choose among different products or approaches. For example, changing the default option for enrollment in retirement plans to automatically enroll new employees while giving them the opportunity to opt out has led to significant increases in plan participation at some organizations. The most effective approach to improving consumers' financial decision making and behavior may be to use a variety of strategies, including financial education.

On October 20, 2011, GAO convened a select group of leaders and experts for a forum to discuss key issues related to financial literacy. These participants, which included representatives of federal, state, and local government agencies; academic experts; nonprofit practitioners; and representatives from the private sector, were selected to represent a range of viewpoints and draw from a variety of backgrounds. In the first session, they discussed current needs related to financial literacy and approaches to setting priorities to meet those needs. In the second session, participants discussed the appropriate roles for the array of government, nonprofit, and private sector entities involved in improving financial literacy and identified strategies for collaborating on and coordinating these efforts. The group then heard from federal public health and nutrition literacy experts and discussed lessons that could be learned from initiatives in these fields to inform their own strategies for influencing and improving consumer financial behaviors. The participants completed the day by discussing GAO's potential role in addressing financial literacy. The forum was structured so that participants could comment on issues openly, although not all participants commented on all topics.

We conducted our work from August 2011 to February 2012 in accordance with all sections of GAO's Quality Assurance Framework that are relevant to our objectives. The framework requires that we plan and perform the engagement to obtain sufficient, appropriate evidence to meet our stated objectives and to discuss any limitations in our work. We believe that the information and data obtained, and the analysis conducted, provide a reasonable basis for any findings and conclusions.

Following is a summary of the discussion among the forum's participants. The summary attempts to capture the ideas and themes that emerged at the forum and the collective discussion of participants at the sessions. The summary does not necessarily represent the views of the organizations whose representatives participated in the forum, including GAO. Participants were given the opportunity to comment on a draft of this summary. Appendix I provides the forum agenda and Appendix II provides a list of the participants. Appendix III lists GAO products on issues related to financial literacy. This report is available on our website at www.gao.gov. For additional information on our work related to financial literacy, please contact Alicia Puente Cackley, Director, Financial Markets and Community Investment, at (202) 512-8678 or cackleya@gao.gov. Key contributors to this report included Jason Bromberg (Assistant Director), Randy Fasnacht, Nina Horowitz, and Roberto Piñero.

I wish to thank all of the participants of this forum for taking the time to share their knowledge and insights on improving financial literacy. I look forward to working with them and others on this important issue in the future.

Gene L. Dodaro
Comptroller General of the United States
February 9, 2012

FINANCIAL LITERACY: HIGHLIGHTS OF THE FORUM DISCUSSION

On October 20, 2011, GAO convened a forum to discuss the needs and priorities in improving financial literacy; roles and responsibilities of and collaboration among the government, nonprofit, and private sectors; lessons learned from federal public health and nutrition literacy initiatives; and GAO's potential role in addressing financial literacy issues. The following summarizes the collective discussion of the forum participants.

Financial Literacy Efforts Should Focus on Key Populations and Skills

Forum participants were asked what areas should receive the most sustained focus of financial literacy efforts in the coming years. Several themes emerged from this conversation.

- Focus on different time periods throughout the life cycle, including kindergarten through 12th grade (K-12) education, college, and the preretirement years. While no clear consensus emerged on a single area of focus, several participants emphasized improving financial literacy among the K-12 population. Financial literacy efforts among the K-12 population have the benefit of schools as an existing distribution system and reach students at an early point in their lives. Other participants suggested focusing on assisting college students manage the financing of their education and accumulated debt. In addition, many participants said efforts should also focus on the workplace to encourage employers to help their employees plan and save for emergencies and their retirement.
- Emphasize special populations that may be particularly vulnerable, including low-income communities, the Hispanic community, and older Americans. One participant expressed the view that the focus should be on the least advantaged among us, in part because the impact of their financial decisions on their lives can be much greater than it is for those with more financial resources. For example, a person whose car breaks down but who lacks sufficient savings for repairs could lose a job as a result. Another participant noted that

Hispanics disproportionately do not participate in employer-sponsored retirement plans, and several agreed about the need to target initiatives to this population to prepare them for retirement. Some participants also discussed the vulnerability of older Americans, with one noting their potentially increased susceptibility to fraud, and another explaining that it can be much harder to recover from financial difficulties later in life.

- Enhance and publicize the importance of basic financial skills and provide more teacher training to support such efforts. Several participants mentioned the need to focus on the importance of havingemergency savings. One participant noted that to effectively teach basic financial literacy there is a need for teachers who are willing and able to teach the subject, yet many teachers lack confidence in their knowledge of the subject matter. Also, some participants said an area of priority should be to create a national media campaign about the importance of financial literacy or to take other steps to raise public awareness about the issue.

Identifying the Most Effective Approaches and Targeting Efforts Accordingly Is Key

One clear theme that emerged from the forum was the need to identify the most effective approaches to improving financial literacy and capability. Participants also highlighted the importance of targeting the right populations, tailoring financial literacy efforts to these populations, improving delivery mechanisms, and leveraging technology.

- *Conduct more research on the effectiveness of different approaches to improving financial literacy.* One participant noted that the increase in high-quality research on this topic in recent years was a positive development. Others noted that the Social Security Administration's recent funding cuts for financial literacy research should be reconsidered. One participant suggested that government, nonprofit, and for-profit entities could develop a shared research agenda that could allow them to share resources.[4]
- *Focus on solutions that change behavior rather than just increase knowledge.* One participant said that financial literacy programs should refocus from simply increasing knowledge to trying to change

behavior. Understanding what behavioral changes result from effective programs and how these changes differ across age, gender, and ethnic groups is important. Several participants noted that automatically enrolling employees in retirement savings plans could be among the most effective tools to prepare people for retirement. But one participant noted that this approach, however successful, needs to be considered carefully in the context of other financial obligations such as managing debt or goals that could be hindered by automatic deductions for retirement, such as saving for emergencies or college tuition.

- *Better tailor products to specific audiences.* According to one participant, financial literacy practitioners have spent a lot of time developing educational materials, but not enough time targeting the people who need more information and matching them up with the appropriate resources. Several participants noted the benefits of integrating financial literacy efforts into existing social service delivery mechanisms, including by using technology more effectively. Some participants cited the need to better understand the most effective approaches to tailoring products for targeted populations. These included whether a trusted resource was delivering the message; whether certain delivery methods such as individual counseling versus classroom training were more effective; and whether key life events, such as the purchase of a home, would be most effective for timing the targeting of different methods.

Employers Can Play an Enhanced Role in Improving the Financial Capability of Their Employees

One of the themes that emerged during the forum was that employers have a key role to play in improving the financial capability of their employees. Participants noted, for example, that employers could encourage their employees to save for emergency purposes and retirement. They also discussed the need to create incentives for employers to support healthy financial behavior by employees. GAO was also encouraged to consider taking additional steps to enhance the financial literacy of its own employees and thus serve as a model for other federal agencies.

Highlight the role of employers in improving the financial capability of their employees. Several forum participants discussed how employers were well positioned to take an active role in improving their employees' financial capability. For example, employees spend a significant amount of time in the workplace, making it a natural place for learning. For instance, they can participate in informative sessions such as "lunch-and-learns" and receive information via company Intranet sites. Participants discussed the fact that many workers do not currently take advantage of employer-sponsored retirement plans because they either do not earn enough to contribute or they need more financial education to understand the benefits of doing so. They proposed actions that employers could take to support greater savings by their employees—for example, by actively encouraging participation in employer-sponsored retirement plans and providing information on alternatives for employees who may not qualify for an employer-based plan, such as part-time staff. Employers could also take steps to facilitate emergency savings for their employees, especially those with lower incomes—for example, by promoting the automatic transfer of a portion of pay into a dedicated savings account.

- Persuade employers of the benefits of financially literate employees. Two participants said that the business case for employer-provided financial literacy recognizes that stress caused by financial issues can reduce productivity and may increase absenteeism and health care costs for employers. Employers thus have an incentive to take an interest in their employees' financial health, just as they do in their employees' physical health through employer-provided health insurance. One participant spoke about a hospital that set up a financial literacy program for its employees to teach them how to buy a home in the local area, and thus benefit from having its workers live nearby. But several participants agreed that employers may need better incentives to take such steps—for example, the government could offer tax incentives for providing financial education to workers or could recognize and honor employers that do exemplary work in financial literacy.
- Establish financial literacy initiatives for government employees. Several participants said that federal agencies should consider establishing financial literacy programs, or enhancing existing ones, for their own employees, as the federal government would serve as a

good testing ground and model for financial literacy initiatives undertaken by other employers. GAO was encouraged to "teach by example"—that is, to establish a financial literacy program for its own employees that could be used as a model for other federal agencies.

The Federal Government Can Leverage Its Unique Role to Promote Financial Literacy

Many forum participants said that the federal government had a unique role to play in promoting greater financial capability. Among other things, the government can make use of its "bully pulpit" and convening power, take advantage of existing delivery mechanisms, and support financial capability efforts through funding, standard setting, and statutory and regulatory changes.

- *Use the "bully pulpit" to draw attention to the importance of promoting greater financial capability.* Many participants agreed on the importance of having the federal government use its unique position to raise awareness of the need for greater financial literacy and capability. They said the government could enhance ongoing efforts to bring visibility to the issue of financial capability and to make it a national priority. Further, they believed encouraging greater financial literacy and capability is an issue that is likely to find support across the political spectrum. Some participants also noted the benefits of having high-level support from the White House and highlighted the President's Advisory Council on Financial Capability. Others noted that First Ladies have often been effective in drawing attention to important issues, such as childhood obesity, drug abuse, and literacy.
- *Leverage the government's convening power.* Participants highlighted the federal government's ability to convene the numerous agencies and entities involved in financial literacy, noting that the government has a powerful ability to bring people together. When a federal agency convenes state, local, private, and nonprofit organizations, participation is likely to be high because those organizations want to be associated with a federal effort. For example, one participant noted that private sector organizations were more likely to want to help with financial literacy efforts if they were asked by the President's Advisory Council on Financial Capability. This ability to convene the key players in the field can also help the

government facilitate setting shared priorities for research. It can also facilitate the sharing of information and best practices on financial literacy among many players.

- *Take advantage of existing points of contact to deliver financial literacy-focused messages.* Participants suggested leveraging existing distribution channels and points of contact between the government and citizens to distribute messages about financial literacy. For example, some participants noted that efforts could be made to deliver additional financial literacy messages through communications from the Social Security Administration, Internal Revenue Service, and Centers for Medicare and Medicaid Services that many American citizens already receive. One important benefit of this approach is that it would entail minimal extra costs to the government. One participant expressed regret at the decision to eliminate the Social Security statement on an annual basis, which he said would have significant negative consequences for financial literacy over the long term.[5]
- *Conduct or fund additional research and data collection to determine the effectiveness of financial literacy programs.* A number of forum participants commented that the federal government should use its resources to conduct or fund additional research into program effectiveness. They pointed out that there are a variety of small programs at the local level, yet it is difficult to know which are most effective at serving their intended population. The federal government could help identify effectiveness, as suggested by one participant, by measuring the impact of programs or policy options for chosen goals, such as an increased savings rate. One participant noted that unlike other organizations, the federal government may be better positioned to collect data that could be useful in evaluating the effectiveness of financial literacy programs; some organizations will share data with the government that they may not share with other entities. The federal government also has a role in funding the training and research of scholars and practitioners in the financial literacy field, according to one participant, which could positively affect the field at relatively low cost.
- *Create standards for financial literacy programs, curriculum content, and teacher training.* There may be a role for the federal government in reviewing, streamlining, or setting standards on the many financial literacy curricula available, according to participants. Several voiced the need for broad-based standards, or a "gold standard," for financial

literacy programs and curricula and for more extensive and standardized teacher training. They noted that standardization could increase the impact and the scale of small programs that served only 100 or 200 people. The standards could include key elements of a financial education program and core competencies of financial education.[6] Participants also discussed the need for better teacher training—for example, one participant cited research showing that teachers were not comfortable with the financial literacy subject area, and another noted that some stakeholders may be looking to the federal government to set guidelines for teacher training.

- *Make legal and regulatory changes to encourage improved financial capability.* Participants discussed opportunities for the federal government to review rules and regulations and to simplify and clarify financial literacy programs and products. Some noted that having to choose from a wide array of financial products—such as retirement accounts, custodian accounts, education savings accounts, and 529 plans—can be overwhelming to consumers, who could benefit if policymakers rethought, or encouraged providers to rethink, the number and nature of such options, according to one participant.[7] Another participant said that the way the Community Reinvestment Act is implemented should be reviewed to ensure that it provides an appropriate amount of support for bank programs that encourage savings.

Opportunities Exist to Increase Coordination and Partnerships within and across Levels of Government and Different Sectors

Participants highlighted that a great deal of progress has been made in recent years in increasing coordination and partnerships among federal, state, and local government agencies; private sector entities; and nonprofits. They encouraged further coordination to help conserve scarce resources and reduce any duplication of effort.

- *Increase coordination and partnership across federal, state, and local government entities.* Many participants discussed ongoing efforts, and opportunities, for coordination among federal, state, and local governments.[8] For example, two state officials called for the Department of the Treasury's help to create a more robust network to facilitate sharing among the state offices.[9] One participant noted the potential coordinating role of the new Bureau of Consumer Financial Protection, while another suggested that the federal government leverage the innovation occurring at the local level by further recognizing and supporting key local efforts. An initiative to connect the unbanked population with financial services, which other cities have replicated in a low-cost way, was an example of such innovation cited by one participant. Another participant suggested creating financial capability councils at the state and city levels, similar to the President's Council on Financial Capability at the federal level, which could serve as "boots on the ground" to improve efforts both nationally and locally. Policy changes, like using waivers to access federal funding, could help state and local governments more easily obtain federal funds for financial literacy programs, according to another participant. Two participants noted that more might be done to reduce unnecessary overlap or duplication among federal financial literacy efforts—for example, one participant questioned whether an online financial capability resource provided by the Bureau of the Public Debt was necessary given the existence of the Federal Deposit Insurance Corporation's Money Smart, a comprehensive financial education curriculum.

- *Continue to build partnerships among the governmental, private, and nonprofit sectors.* Some participants noted that these different sectors would benefit from more of a shared agenda and resources, which would allow them to more effectively use scarce funds. One participant noted that nonprofit entities can lead the way in developing new effective approaches, and another added that nonprofits can test and prove new concepts and pilot initiatives that are too risky for the government or private sector. A different participant said that there needs to be a better infrastructure in place between private sector and nonprofit organizations to bring those innovative ideas from the test and concept phase to actual implementation on a large scale. The nonprofit sector can also benefit from leadership by government or the private sector to show the value of different approaches. For example, one participant noted that the nonprofit sector would be bolstered by government and private sector leadership showing the value of housing counseling, which some view as a component of financial literacy.

Financial Literacy Efforts Can Be Informed by Lessons from Other Efforts to Improve Consumer Behaviors

The federal government has experience trying to educate consumers and influence their behavior in areas other than financial matters. During an afternoon session of the forum, Dr. Linda Harris, the Acting Deputy Director of the Office of Disease Prevention and Health Promotion at the Department of Health and Human Services (HHS), gave a presentation on the department's efforts to improve health outcomes. Dr. Rajen Anand, the Executive Director of the Center for Nutrition Policy and Promotion at the Department of Agriculture, and his colleague John Webster, spoke about improving consumer choices about food and nutrition.

Dr. Harris's presentation described how health literacy—the degree to which individuals have the capacity to obtain, communicate, process, and understand basic health information and services to make appropriate health decisions—is critical to avoiding many negative health outcomes. She described an HHS working group that developed a national action plan to improve health literacy.[10] Her agency has also worked to create an effective website to help consumers make informed choices. Dr. Harris also explained that the Plain Writing Act of 2010—requiring clear government communication that the public can understand and use—has been an important part of a strategy to improve health literacy and outcomes.

Dr. Anand's presentation focused on efforts to foster positive dietary decision making and behavior change. He described a number of factors that affect consumer behavior around diet and nutrition, including individual factors such as age, gender, socioeconomic status, race and ethnicity; environmental factors such as what type of food is available at school, work, and home; and social and cultural factors such as belief systems about food, religious traditions, and body image. Dr. Anand also discussed his agency's role in the formulation of the "MyPlate" food plate to replace the food pyramid.

During a question-and-answer session following the presentation, participants discussed:

- *Parallels between financial literacy and health and nutrition literacy.* Participants noted similarities between health and financial literacy efforts. Both efforts are challenged by how difficult it is to influence people to change their behaviors. Also, poor health literacy and financial literacy can both have significant negative consequences to individuals and families. Finally, both could benefit from a focus on prevention—that is, seeking to prevent poor health outcomes or financial problems in the first place.

- *Possible creation of something akin to MyPlate for financial literacy.* The Department of Agriculture's MyPlate provides a visual representation of the nutritionally appropriate balance among food groups. One participant began a discussion about creating something similar to the food plate to emphasize certain key elements of financial literacy: earning, saving, investing, borrowing, spending, and protecting. Participants discussed the benefits of such an effort, such as creating a simple visual reference point for discussing financial literacy.
- *Difficulties of measuring effectiveness.* Dr. Harris and Dr. Anand discussed how research on the effectiveness of their programs has been limited but will hopefully increase over time. One participant discussed the National Health and Nutrition Examination Survey—a program of studies designed to assess the health and nutritional status of adults and children in the United States—and the potential benefit of such a survey on financial literacy.[11] Another participant noted that one difference between financial literacy and health and nutrition literacy is that the latter has a large number of researchers and an extensive and well-funded body of research and academic journals devoted to the topic.
- *Value of the web, social media, and other outreach efforts.* Dr. Harris and Mr. Webster both discussed online tools their agencies created that allow people to enter their age and other information to get targeted information about health and nutrition. Mr. Webster also discussed how his agency has created a network of more than 4,000 community partners, including churches and scout organizations to help get out the word about good nutrition.
- *Importance of policy changes to supplement literacy efforts.* One participant described how past campaigns to affect behavior have to a great extent been aided by adoption of policies that change incentives for behavior, such as laws banning smoking and requiring the use of seat belts. The participant also noted that there is little evidence on the effectiveness of information campaigns that do not include accompanying changes in incentives—for example, the impact of the

dairy industry's "Got Milk" campaign on milk consumption is unclear.

GAO Can Play a Role in Improving Financial Literacy

During the final hour of the forum, participants shared their views on how GAO or the Comptroller General might support or raise awareness about financial literacy, or partner with others to do so. Participants suggested that, as part of its traditional role in studying federal oversight of financial markets and products, GAO should conduct studies on a number of topics including emergency savings, financial planners, and retirement accounts. In addition, the participants suggested the following:

- *GAO could facilitate or conduct research on effective programs.* Many participants said that GAO might conduct research—or continue to summarize existing research—on effective approaches and delivery methods to improving financial literacy, and highlight particularly effective programs. Another participant said GAO could help improve the effectiveness of financial literacy efforts by identifying programs that may be duplicative. GAO could also use its ongoing studies to raise awareness of existing data sources and encourage agencies to share such resources. Finally, GAO could highlight best practices, standards, or metrics that could be adopted more broadly.
- *GAO could establish a financial literacy initiative for its employees to serve as a model agency.* Participants suggested that GAO could develop an employee financial literacy initiative that could be a model for other federal agencies. One participant described efforts in the private sector to create financial literacy curricula for their employees. One focus of such an effort by GAO, said another participant, could be newer staff who may have considerable student loan debt to manage.
- *GAO can help identify and encourage opportunities to provide financial education where the federal government is already interacting with individuals.* Some participants suggested that as part of its ongoing oversight of federal agencies, GAO could help identify effective access points at which agencies already regularly interact with consumers. For example, GAO could review ways the federal

government could better leverage the distribution of financial information already taking place at agencies such as the Internal Revenue Service, the Social Security Administration, and the Departments of Labor and Education.

- *GAO should continue to draw attention to the importance of financial literacy, including by convening experts.* Many participants said that GAO should continue to use its unique position to draw attention to the issue of financial literacy and convene groups similar to the forum. One participant noted that the field will benefit from the Comptroller General's involvement in this topic, while another said it is useful to have a neutral third party such as GAO bring together financial literacy stakeholders to address the issues.

APPENDIX I: FORUM AGENDA

Financial Literacy: Strengthening Partnerships in Challenging Times A Forum Convened by Comptroller General Gene L. Dodaro U.S. Government Accountability Office

Thursday, October 20, 2011

Agenda

8:30 a.m.	Continental Breakfast	McCarl Room, 7C21
9:00 a.m.	Opening Session	Staats Briefing Room, 7C13
	-Welcome	Gene L. Dodaro
	-Personal introductions	Comptroller General of the United States
	-Overview of agenda	
9:20 a.m.	Current and Future Needs, Priorities,	Moderator:
	and Challenges	Barbara Bovbjerg
		Managing Director
		Education, Workforce, and Income Security, GAO
10:30 a.m.	Break	
10:40 a.m.	Roles, Coordination, and Collaboration	Moderator:

		Orice Williams Brown
		Managing Director
		Financial Markets and Community Investment, GAO
11:50 a.m.	Break	
12:15 p.m.	Working Lunch—	Moderator:
	Lessons from Efforts to Influence Other	Susan Offutt
	Consumer Behaviors	Chief Economist, GAO
1:30 p.m.	Break	
1:40 p.m.	GAO's Role	Moderator:
		Gene L. Dodaro
2:30 p.m.	Wrap-up	Gene L. Dodaro
2:45 p.m.	Adjournment	

APPENDIX II: FORUM PARTICIPANTS

Rajen Anand	Executive Director, Center for Nutrition Policy and Promotion Department of Agriculture
Theodore J. Beck	President and CEO National Endowment for Financial Education
Barbara Bovbjerg	Managing Director, Education, Workforce, and Income Security Government Accountability Office
Orice Williams Brown	Managing Director, Financial Markets and Community Investment Government Accountability Office
Judy J. Chapa	Vice President of Community Services The Financial Services Roundtable
Gene L. Dodaro	Comptroller General of the United States
Heidi Goldberg	Program Director, Early Childhood and Family Economic Success, Institute for

	Youth, Education, and Families National League of Cities
Linda Harris	Acting Deputy Director, Office of Disease Prevention and Health Promotion Department of Health and Human ServicesGail HillebrandAssociate Director of Consumer Education and Engagement Bureau of Consumer Financial Protection
Jeanne Hogarth	Manager, Consumer and Community Affairs Board of Governors of the Federal Reserve System
Susan C. Keating	President and CEO National Foundation for Credit Counseling
Laura Levine	President and CEO Jump$tart Coalition for Personal Financial Literacy
Annamaria Lusardi	Professor of Accountancy and Economics George Washington University School of Business
Cathleen Mahon	Executive Director and Deputy Commissioner for Financial Empowerment, Office of Financial Empowerment New York City Department of Consumer Affairs
Dave Mancl	Director, Office of Financial Literacy State of Wisconsin
Brenda McDaniel	Program Analyst, Financial Readiness Program, Office of Family Policy Department of Defense
Brandee McHale	Chief Operating Officer Citi Foundation
Susan Offut t	Chief Economist Government Accountability Office
Gary John Previts	Distinguished University Professor and Chair, Department of Accountancy Case Western Reserve University
Luke W. Reynolds	Chief, Outreach and Program Development, Division of Depositor and Consumer Protection Federal Deposit Insurance Corporation

Mary Rosenkrans	Director, Office of Financial Education, Department of Banking State of Pennsylvania
Dallas Salisbury	President and CEO Employee Benefit Research Institute
Lori Schock	Director, Office of Investor Education and Advocacy Securities and Exchange Commission
Carrie Schwab-Pomerantz	President Charles Schwab Foundation
David A. Weaver	Acting Associate Commissioner, Office of Retirement Policy Social Security Administration
John Webster	Director of Public Affairs, Center for Nutrition Policy and Promotion Department of Agriculture
Lauren E. Willis	Professor of Law Loyola Law School
Joshua Wright	Acting Director, Office of Financial Education and Financial Access Department of the Treasury

Appendix III: Related GAO Products

Financial Education and Counseling Pilot Program. GAO-11-737R. Washington, D.C.: July 27, 2011.

Cost and Legal Authority for Selected Financial Literacy Programs and Activities. GAO-11-781R. Washington, D.C.: July 13, 2011.

Financial Literacy: A Federal Certification Process for Providers Would Pose Challenges. GAO-11-614. Washington, D.C.: June 28, 2011.

Financial Literacy: The Federal Government's Role in Empowering Americans to Make Sound Financial Choices. GAO-11-504T. Washington, D.C.: April 12, 2011.

Opportunities to Reduce Potential Duplication in Government Programs, Save Tax Dollars, and Enhance Revenue. GAO-11-318SP. Washington, D.C.: March 1, 2011.

Consumer Finance: Factors Affecting the Financial Literacy of Individuals with Limited English Proficiency. GAO-10-518. Washington, D.C.: May 21, 2010.

(Spanish Language Summary: Finanzas del Consumidor: Factores que Afectan la Educacion Financiera de las Personas con Conocimientos Limitados del Ingles. GAO-10-869, August 4, 2010.)

Financial Literacy and Education Commission: Progress Made in Fostering Partnerships, but National Strategy Remains Largely Descriptive Rather Than Strategic. GAO-09-638T. Washington, D.C.: April 29, 2009.

Financial Literacy and Education Commission: Further Progress Needed to Ensure an Effective National Strategy. GAO-07-777T. Washington, D.C.: April 30, 2007.

Increasing Financial Literacy in America. GAO-07-284CG. Washington, D.C.: December 11, 2006.

Financial Literacy and Education Commission: Further Progress Needed to Ensure an Effective National Strategy. GAO-07-100. Washington, D.C.: December 4, 2006.

Credit Reporting Literacy: Consumers Understood the Basics but Could Benefit from Targeted Educational Efforts. GAO-05-223. Washington, D.C.: March 16, 2005.

Highlights of a GAO Forum: The Federal Government's Role in Improving Financial Literacy. GAO-05-93SP. Washington, D.C.: November 15, 2004.

End Notes

[1] The Financial Literacy and Education Commission has described "financial literacy" as the ability to make informed judgments and to take effective actions regarding current and future use and management of money. It has described "financial capability" as an individual's capacity, based on knowledge, skills, and access, to manage financial resources effectively.

[2] GAO, Highlights of a GAO Forum: The Federal Government's Role in Improving Financial Literacy, GAO-05-93SP (Washington, D.C.: Nov. 15, 2004).

[3] In 2003, Congress created the multiagency Financial Literacy and Education Commission, which was charged with, among other things, developing a national strategy to promote financial literacy and education, coordinating federal efforts, and identifying areas of overlap and duplication. Pub. L. No. 108-159, §§ 511-519 (codified at 20 U.S.C. §§ 9701–9708).

[4] The Financial Literacy and Education Commission's 2011 National Strategy set as a goal to "identify, enhance, and share effective practices," including encouraging research on effective strategies for affecting consumer behavior, establishing a research clearinghouse, and supporting program evaluation efforts. In October 2008, the Departments of the Treasury and Agriculture convened a National Research Symposium on Financial Literacy and Education that sought to identify gaps in the research and develop research priorities.

[5] The Social Security Administration announced in March of 2011 that as a result of budget cuts it was suspending the provision of annual or other Social Security benefit estimates by mail.

[6] Federal agencies have already taken several steps to address standards and competencies. For example, in 2004, the Department of the Treasury's Office of Financial Education and Financial Access published a list of the elements of a successful financial education program, and in August 2010, the Financial Literacy and Education Commission developed a set of "core competencies" that define what consumers should know to make informed decisions about their personal finances. The commission's 2011 national strategy sets an objective to develop guidelines related to curriculum development, delivery methods, and other areas that could be used by financial education providers.

[7] A 529 plan, legally known as a "qualified tuition program," is a tax-advantaged savings plan authorized by Section 529 of the Internal Revenue Code and designed to encourage saving for future college costs.

[8] GAO has examined successful approaches to federal agency collaboration. See GAO, Results-Oriented Government: Practices That Can Help Enhance and Sustain Collaboration Among Federal Agencies, GAO-06-15 (Washington, D.C.: Oct. 21, 2005).

[9] In April 2007, the Financial Literacy and Education Commission created the National Financial Education Network to facilitate and advance financial education at the state and local levels. Among other things, the network has developed a web-based database to share information across entities and held national conferences.

[10] U.S. Department of Health and Human Services, Office of Disease Prevention and Health Promotion. National Action Plan to Improve Health Literacy (Washington, D.C.: 2010).

[11] Among the existing efforts that have sought to assess Americans' financial literacy is the National Financial Capability Study conducted by the Investor Education Foundation of the Financial Industry Regulatory Authority, Inc. Financial Capability in the United States, Initial Report of Research Findings from the 2009 National Survey, A Component of the National Financial Capability Study (New York, N.Y.: Dec. 1, 2009).

In: Financial Literacy Forums
Editor: Caroline Holland

ISBN: 978-1-63484-337-9

Chapter 3

THE FEDERAL GOVERNMENT'S ROLE IN IMPROVING FINANCIAL LITERACY*

United States Government Accountability Office

WHY GAO CONVENED THIS FORUM

Research has shown that many Americans lack the knowledge of basic personal economics they need to make informed financial judgments and manage their money effectively. Yet financial literacy is increasingly important in a world where consumers must choose from an array of complicated financial products and services and employees must take on more responsibility for their retirement savings. Title V of the Fair and Accurate Credit Transactions Act of 2003, known as the Financial Literacy and Education Improvement Act, created the Financial Literacy and Education Commission, comprised of 20 federal agencies, and charged it with coordinating federal efforts and developing a national strategy to promote financial literacy.

The act also mandated that GAO report on recommendations for improving financial literacy among consumers. To help in developing our work, on July 28, 2004, GAO hosted a forum on the role of the federal government in improving financial literacy. Forum participants included experts in financial literacy and education from federal and state agencies, the

* This is an edited, reformatted and augmented version of a report, GAO-05-93SP, issued by the Government Accountability Office, dated November 2014.

financial industry, nonprofit organizations, and academic institutions. Participants discussed the topics federal efforts should cover, populations that should be targeted, methods of delivering information, and the role of program evaluation.

WHAT PARTICIPANTS SAID

Forum participants offered a number of suggestions regarding the federal government's role in improving Americans' financial literacy:

- *The federal government should serve as a leader.* The federal government should use its influence, authority, and "bully pulpit" to make financial literacy a national priority. However, given that a wide array of state, local, nonprofit and private organizations already provide financial education, the federal government's role should largely be supportive, filling the gaps left by others and serving as an unbiased source of information.
- *Increased public-private partnerships and interagency coordination are needed.* Partnerships between federal agencies and other organizations are the best way to use scarce resources efficiently, facilitate the sharing of best practices, and help federal agencies reach targeted populations at the community level. In addition, federal financial literacy efforts should be integrated across agencies and consolidated to focus on those agencies with the most expertise and best track records in this area.
- *Consumers need financial information on a broad range of topics.* Among the most important topics for financial education are basic skills—such as budgeting, planning, and managing money—as well as information on saving for retirement, investing, and managing credit. Financial education should be delivered at "teachable moments" when the information is applicable to a person's life. Participants' views varied on the need to incorporate into financial education broader issues such as the implications to individuals of the budget deficit and long-term fiscal challenges facing the nation.
- *A variety of methods are needed to deliver financial education effectively.* Participants said that the federal government should sponsor a major media campaign with a clear and simple message and

find ways to ensure that existing financial education materials are more widely disseminated. Participants also emphasized the importance of personal interaction—such as one-on-one counseling—and of including financial education in school curriculums. To this end, they said the U.S. Department of Education needs to deepen its commitment to financial education.

- *Financial literacy programs need to be evaluated.* Program evaluation ideally should assess outcomes, such as the impact on participants' personal savings. The federal government can facilitate others' evaluation efforts by developing or supporting standardized evaluation tools, serving as a national clearinghouse for evaluation efforts, and disseminating best practices.

* * *

November 15, 2004

The Honorable Richard C. Shelby
Chairman

The Honorable Paul S. Sarbanes
Ranking Minority Member
Committee on Banking, Housing, and Urban Affairs
United States Senate

The Honorable Michael G. Oxley
Chairman
The Honorable Barney Frank Ranking Minority Member
Committee on Financial Services House of Representatives

Subject: *Highlights of a GAO Forum: The Federal Government's Role in Improving Financial Literacy*

Faced with growing evidence that large numbers of Americans lack knowledge about basic personal economics and financial planning, policymakers and others have begun to focus increasing attention on the state of financial literacy in the United States. Financial literacy can be defined as the ability to make informed judgments and to take effective actions regarding the current and future use and management of money. It includes the ability to understand financial choices, plan for the future, spend wisely, and manage the challenges that come with life events such as a job loss and saving for retirement or a child's education. A lack of financial literacy affects consumers' economic well-being and security in a variety of ways. Poor money management and financial decision making can lower a family's standard of living and interfere with crucial long-term goals, such as buying a home and financing retirement.

Financial literacy has broader public policy implications as well. The financial markets work best when consumers understand how financial services providers and products work and know how to choose among them. Further, informed consumers can help discipline markets by choosing appropriate financial investments, products, and services. In addition, our income tax system requires citizens to have an adequate understanding of the tax system and financial matters in general. Educated consumers are also essential to well-functioning retirement systems—consumers must understand, for example, that Social Security is not intended to be an individual's only source of retirement income. Finally, financial literacy is important in ensuring that Americans who receive public assistance successfully transition to greater self-sufficiency.

However, there is evidence that financial literacy in America needs to be improved. For example, a 2003 national survey by AARP of consumers aged 45 and older found that they often lacked knowledge of basic financial and investment terms. Only about half of respondents, for instance, reported knowing that diversification of investments reduces risk. Similarly, in a recent survey of 4,000 high school seniors conducted by the Jump$tart Coalition for Personal Financial Literacy, students correctly answered an average of only 52 percent of questions on basic personal finances. Yet a number of trends have emerged in recent years that underscore the importance of financial literacy in everyday life.

- Consumers are faced with a wider and increasingly complicated array of options for managing their personal finances and selecting investments and credit products.
- Technological advances have increased the capacity for targeted marketing to consumers, potentially increasing some consumers' vulnerability to predatory lenders and other unscrupulous providers of financial services.

- Consumers are increasingly responsible for their own retirement savings, with traditional defined-benefit retirement plans becoming increasingly rare.
- The personal saving rate has fallen dramatically, declining from nearly 7 percent of gross domestic product in the 1970s and 1980s to around 2 percent in recent years.
- Household debt as a percentage of income hovers at record high levels. In addition, bankruptcy rates have more than quadrupled in the past 20 years.

Finally, I believe that a clear understanding of the country's overall financial condition and future fiscal outlook is an indispensable part of true financial literacy. The financial futures of the American people are shaped not only by their own personal planning and individual investments but also by the fiscal choices made in Washington. The official U.S. gross debt now stands at more than $7 trillion, and that does not include tens of trillions in unfunded Social Security and Medicare benefits, veterans' health care, and a range of other commitments and contingencies. Due to current demographic trends, rising health care costs, and other factors, we face the possibility of decades of mounting deficits, which left unchecked will threaten our economic and national security, while also adversely affecting the quality of life and opportunities available to future generations. Americans must be aware of these developments in planning for their own financial futures, since, for example, we can no longer assume that current federal entitlement programs will continue indefinitely in their present form.

Currently, about 20 different federal agencies operate about 30 different programs or initiatives related to financial literacy. In addition, federal agencies often partner with the multitude of nonprofit, industry, state, and local entities that sponsor, fund, or operate their own financial literacy initiatives. These efforts cover a wide variety of topics, target a range of audiences, and include classroom curricula, print materials, Web sites, broadcast media, and individual counseling. In Title V of the Fair and Accurate Credit Transactions Act of 2003, known as the Financial Literacy and Education Improvement Act,[1] Congress created the Financial Literacy and Education Commission (the Commission). The Commission is made up of 20 federal agencies and is charged with developing a national strategy to promote financial literacy and education for all Americans. The Commission is also charged with coordinating financial education efforts among federal agencies and between the federal government and state and local governments, nonprofit organizations, and private enterprises. The Commission is to identify areas of overlap and duplication among federal financial literacy activities.

The act also mandated that GAO report on recommendations for improving financial literacy among consumers.[2] On July 28, 2004, GAO hosted a forum to develop recommendations on the role of the federal government in improving financial literacy among consumers. The forum's participants included a select group of individuals with expertise in financial literacy and education. They included representatives of federal and state agencies, the financial industry, nonprofit organizations, and academic institutions. Participants were asked to consider the appropriate role of the federal government in financial literacy, particularly in relation to the role of state and local government agencies, nonprofit organizations, and financial services institutions. Participants discussed how the federal government could coordinate its efforts and partner with others more effectively. They also discussed the appropriate topics, target populations, and methods of delivery for federal financial education efforts and the role of program evaluation.

Following is a summary of the discussion among the forum participants. Appendix I provides a list of the participants. Appendix II lists GAO products on issues related to financial literacy.

I wish to thank all of the participants of this forum for taking the time to share their knowledge and insights on financial education and on the role of the federal government in improving America's financial literacy. I look forward to working with them and others on this important issue in the future.

David M. Walker
Comptroller General of the United States

FINANCIAL LITERACY: HIGHLIGHTS OF FORUM DISCUSSION

On July 28, 2004, GAO hosted a forum to develop recommendations on the role of the federal government in improving financial literacy among consumers. Participants discussed the federal government's overall role in financial literacy as well as issues of coordination and partnership, topics for financial education, target populations, methods of delivery, and the role of program evaluation. The following summarizes the collective discussion of the forum participants as well as subsequent comments received from participants based on a draft of this report.

THE FEDERAL GOVERNMENT SHOULD SERVE AS A LEADER IN EFFORTS TO IMPROVE FINANCIAL LITERACY

Forum participants discussed the appropriate role for the federal government in improving financial literacy. They emphasized that the federal government should use its influence and authority to make financial literacy a national priority. In large part, its role should be to fill gaps left in the financial education efforts of the nonprofit and private sectors.

- *The federal government should serve as a leader.* Participants emphasized that for a federal financial literacy effort to be successful, the driving force must come from the highest levels, such as the President or a cabinet secretary. Efforts to make financial literacy a prominent national issue can not come solely from the grassroots level but require exercising the "bully pulpit" of federal leadership. Further, this leadership must have a strong enough passion about financial literacy to keep the nation focused on the issue. One participant said that an important figure or agency must take the issue of financial literacy as a "life purpose," noting that the success or failure of federal efforts could depend on the effectiveness of the Department of the Treasury's Office of Financial Education. Some participants noted that making financial literacy a sustained priority would be difficult, particularly given the federal government's current focus on terrorism and foreign issues. Participants were complimentary of Congress's creation of the Financial Literacy and Education Commission. However, one participant noted that given the large number of issues that Congress takes up, it can be a challenge to keep its attention focused on any one issue for an extended period of time.
- *The federal government's role in financial education should be to fill the gaps left by others and serve as an unbiased source of information.* Participants said that the federal government exists to serve its citizens by addressing a broad set of needs. With regard to improving financial literacy, the government should direct its efforts to the gaps in coverage—topics and populations that are not being

addressed adequately by the financial education initiatives of the nonprofit and private sectors. Some participants noted that while the corporate world has some very good financial education initiatives, the private sector is ultimately driven by the bottom line and may not always be motivated to devote resources to broad-based, noncommercial consumer financial education. For this reason, it is important for the government to serve as an objective and unbiased source of information, particularly in terms of helping consumers make wise decisions about the selection of financial products and services. Many participants also said that consumer protection is a natural role for the government, especially in those cases where the private sector does not have a vested financial interest of its own at stake. One participant noted that the federal government should ensure that the mandated disclosures on many financial products, such as mutual fund prospectuses and mortgage forms, are useful and readable—that is, that they actually serve to help inform and protect consumers rather than simply protect companies against legal liability.

Increased Public-Private Partnerships and Interagency Coordination Are Needed

Federal agencies often partner with nonprofit and industry organizations that sponsor, fund, or operate financial literacy initiatives. Participants said that such partnerships are essential and suggested measures the federal government can take to facilitate them. Participants also recommended that the federal government improve coordination of the many financial literacy programs that exist among multiple federal agencies. They suggested that the federal effort be streamlined to avoid duplication and concentrate resources on those federal agencies best equipped to provide financial education.

- *Public-private partnership is key.* Participants said that there are many benefits to the development of partnerships involving the federal government, the states, industry groups, and nonprofit organizations in efforts to improve financial literacy. They noted that partnering
- makes the most efficient use of scarce resources,
- facilitates the sharing of best practices among different organizations,

- helps the federal government reach targeted populations via community-based organizations at the grassroots level, and
- facilitates coordination of the increasing number of financial literacy programs that exist nationwide.

Participants felt that in general the federal government should seek to build on rather than duplicate the financial education efforts that have been undertaken at the community level. Finally, organizations should understand their comparative advantage. For example, one participant noted that while the Federal Reserve System is good at creating financial education materials, community groups are good at distributing them. With effective partnerships, each organization has a role and can focus on what it does best.

- *The federal government can take measures to increase public-private partnerships.* Two participants said that the federal government should provide stronger incentives to corporate America to support financial literacy programs, because the private sector will not necessarily provide such programs otherwise. The Community Reinvestment Act is one example of the federal government's efforts to encourage financial institutions to support financial literacy in communities they serve.[3] One participant also cited the Department of Defense's Financial Readiness Campaign as an example of effective partnering, noting that the campaign brought together 26 agencies and organizations from the private and public sectors to help improve financial literacy among members of the military. Another participant cited Jump$tart as an effective model of partnership because it brought together a variety of players.[4] One suggested that the federal government consider more collaboration with financial planners, who have direct contact with consumers and thus are well positioned to provide financial information. Because financial planners and other private parties often sell financial services and products, however, public agencies need to establish ground rules for such collaborations that address any potential conflicts of interest. One participant also said the federal government should facilitate more intergovernmental partnering. States and localities tend to look to the federal government for leadership, and federal agencies can do more to bring together state treasurers, state securities commissioners, governors, and others in support of efforts to improve financial literacy.

- *Federal interagency and intra-agency efforts should be better coordinated.* Participants generally believed that the federal government is doing good work providing financial education and promoting financial literacy, but some were concerned about the possibility of duplication among programs and the number of federal agencies involved in these efforts. It was felt that the federal financial literacy effort should be streamlined so that agencies with the most expertise and best track records in this area would be doing the work. One participant stated some federal programs were being managed by individuals with insufficient background in financial education issues. Another participant noted that the Department of the Treasury's Office of Financial Education, created in 2002, represented a good first step because it served as a central point of contact for federal financial literacy efforts. Participants also believed that the federal Financial Literacy and Education Commission would play a beneficial role in coordinating federal activities. The Commission, participants said, would raise the profile of the financial literacy issue among agency leadership, coordinate the work of multiple federal agencies, and create an overall federal strategy for improving financial literacy. One participant also noted that coordination of financial literacy efforts *within* federal agencies needed to be improved. As an example, the participant cited an incident involving staff who were working on a financial literacy initiative, unaware that a similar effort was under way elsewhere in the agency.

CONSUMERS REQUIRE FINANCIAL INFORMATION ON A BROAD RANGE OF TOPICS

What topics should federal efforts to promote financial literacy emphasize? Forum participants said that basic money management skills are most essential and that individuals should be educated on meeting future financial obligations. Investment and retirement savings were also commonly cited as important topics. But participants views varied on the need to incorporate into financial education broader issues such as the budget deficit and long-term fiscal challenges facing the nation.

Consumers need some basic knowledge if they are to make responsible and informed financial decisions. Participants agreed that federal financial literacy efforts should first and foremost aim to give consumers the basic financial knowledge and skills needed to make responsible financial decisions. Budgeting, saving, money management, and basic financial planning were frequently cited as the most essential topics for a financial education strategy. Participants also thought that consumers would benefit from more education on credit, including the cost of credit and how to use and manage credit responsibly. Two participants discussed the importance of encouraging consumers to do more research into products and services before making a purchase, noting that many consumers make imprudent decisions because they fail to comparison shop. Several participants also cited the importance of providing education on consumer protection issues, especially on avoiding fraud.

The federal government should prepare consumers for future financial challenges. Participants said that the federal government should educate individuals on meeting future financial obligations such as paying for health care and saving for retirement. For example, participants said that consumers need more information on planning for health care expenses in an era of rising medical costs and increasing longevity. One participant commented that the best way to prepare consumers for a financially sound future is to help them find and retain employment. As part of this effort, youth and new immigrants should be educated on the nation's entrepreneurial business culture so that they are better prepared to enter the workforce.

Investing and saving for retirement should be an important focus of financial education. In an era when employees are increasingly expected to take responsibility for funding their retirements, several participants stressed the importance of educating consumers on investing wisely and saving for retirement. Participants said that consumers need instruction on basic investment principles, such as the comparative risks of different types of investments and the need to diversify investments to reduce risk. In addition, consumers need more information on saving to accumulate enough retirement funds to last the duration of their lives. One participant encouraged the federal government to reach workers who are on the cusp of retirement with information on making the transition from saving for retirement to living off of investment income and Social Security. Several participants recommended that the federal government use the annual statements that the Social Security Administration sends to most Americans as a means of delivering some of this financial education.

Describes government, industry, and nonprofit efforts to provide consumer education on predatory home mortgage lending. Finds that consumer education efforts in general are useful, but that their ability to deter predatory lending may be limited by several factors, including the complexity of mortgage transactions and the difficulty of reaching the target audience.

Military Personnel: DOD Needs More Data to Address Financial and Health Care Issues Affecting Reservists. GAO-03-1004. Washington, D.C.: September 10, 2003.

Describes the Department of Defense's personal financial management services and education provided to reservists and their families. Finds that the department is taking steps to improve personal financial management, but has not assessed the financial well-being of reserve families, assessed the impact of reservists' financial problems on mission readiness, or determined how to tailor its programs to reservists.

Private Pensions: Participants Need Information on Risks They Face in Managing Pension Assets at and during Retirement. GAO-03-810. Washington, D.C.: July 29, 2003.

Describes the information that pension plans make available to participants at retirement and identifies a range of actions to help retiring participants preserve their pension and retirement savings plan assets. Suggests that Congress consider requiring plan sponsors to provide a notice on risks that individuals face when managing their income and expenditures at and during retirement.

Electronic Transfers: Use by Federal Payment Recipients Has Increased but Obstacles to Greater Participation Remain. GAO-02-913. Washington, D.C.: September 12, 2002.

Discusses ways of increasing the use of electronic fund transfers for benefit payments made through the Social Security Administration and other programs. Briefly describes efforts by government, industry, and nonprofit organizations to publicize the use of electronic fund transfers, often as part of broader financial literacy programs.

Private Pensions: Participants Need Information on the Risks of Investing in Employer Securities and the Benefits of Diversification. GAO-02-943. Washington, D.C.: September 6, 2002.

Finds that employees can face significant risks when investing in employer securities through employer-sponsored retirement plans, and describes the regulatory provisions for disclosures to participants of such plans. Suggests that Congress consider requiring plan sponsors to provide an investment education notice containing basic information on risk management and the importance of diversification.

Retirement Saving: Opportunities to Improve DOL's SAVER Act Campaign. GAO-01-634. Washington, D.C.: June 26, 2001.

Reviews the Department of Labor's Retirement Savings Education Campaign, which seeks to educate individuals about the importance of saving for retirement. Finds that the department has not attempted to assess the extent to which its outreach efforts have increased the public's knowledge and understanding of retirement saving and makes recommendations related to such an evaluation.

Consumer Finance: College Students and Credit Cards. GAO-01-773. Washington, D.C.: June 20, 2001.

Describes credit card issuers' practices for marketing to college students and universities' policies and practices on credit card solicitation. Discusses the advantages and disadvantages that credit cards present to college students. Includes description of financial education efforts by some universities, particularly those responding to concerns about aggressive credit card solicitations.

Social Security: Capital Markets and Educational Issues Associated With Individual Accounts. GAO/GGD-99-115. Washington, D.C.: June 28, 1999.

Discusses the public education efforts that would be needed should the Social Security program be modified to include individual investment accounts. Finds that a broad-based educational effort would be required to educate individuals on making appropriate investment decisions and to protect against misinformation.

End Notes

[1] Pub. L. No. 108-159, Title V, 117 Stat. 2003 (codified at 20 U.S.C. §§ 9701 – 08).

[2] See 20 U.S.C. § 9706(b). This provision also mandated GAO to assess the extent of consumers' knowledge and awareness of credit reports, credit scores, and the dispute resolution process. This issue will be addressed in a forthcoming GAO report.

[3] The Community Reinvestment Act (CRA) holds banks and savings institutions accountable for meeting the credit needs of all communities they are chartered to serve, including low- and moderate-income communities. Under the legislation, federal banking agencies periodically evaluate banks to ensure that they are attentive to community needs. A bank's efforts to improve financial literacy in the community may be taken into account in assessing CRA performance.

Q

R

S

T

U

V

W

Y